Weather
and the
Seasons

Editor **Violet Peto**
Project Art Editor **Victoria Palastanga**
Producer **John Casey**
Senior Producer, Pre-Production **Luca Frassinetti**
Jacket Coordinator **Francesca Young**
Managing Editor **Penny Smith**
Managing Art Editor **Mabel Chan**
Creative Director **Helen Senior**
Publisher **Sarah Larter**

**Produced for DK
by Dynamo Ltd**

First published in Great Britain in 2019 by
Dorling Kindersley Limited
80 Strand, London WC2R 0RL

A CIP catalogue record for this book is available
from the British Library.
ISBN: 978-0-2413-1220-9
Printed in China.

A WORLD OF IDEAS
SEE ALL THERE IS TO KNOW

www.dk.com

Parents

This book is packed with activities for your little ones to enjoy. We want you all to have a great time, but please be safe and sensible – especially when you're doing anything that might *be* dangerous (or messy!). Have fun.

Contents

What is weather?

Outside there is coldness, warmness, wind, rain, and snow. This is all **weather**.

In the air

Weather happens in the air around us every day. Clouds drop rain and snow in the air.

Favourite weather

What kind of weather do you like best? Do you like sunny days that are good for swimming, or snowy days that are good for sledging?

You can feel air moving around you when it's windy.

Night **Day**

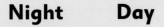

Warm or cold?

It is often colder at night, when the Sun goes down. In cold weather the air around us feels chilly. In sunny weather it can feel warm. How warm or cold the air feels is called its temperature.

Clothes help us stay warm, cool, or dry in different weather.

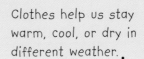

Weather wheel

Make this wonderful **wheel** and you can become a real **weather forecaster**.

Use a ribbon to hang the wheel up.

Every day, turn the arrow to show what the weather is like. It's sunny today!

1

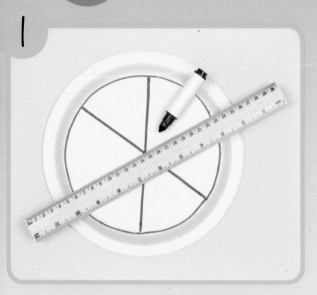

Draw a large circle on the paper plate.
Use a ruler and pen to divide the circle
into six sections.

2

Draw a picture in each section
to show different types of weather.
Colour in your weather wheel.

3

Next squeeze on glitter glue to make your
pictures sparkle. Leave the plate to dry.

4

Ask an adult to help.

Cut out a card arrow. Make a hole in
the arrow and in the centre of the plate.
Fasten on the arrow with a split pin.

Seasons

The weather **changes** at **different times** through the year. These times are called the **seasons**.

Four seasons

In most areas of the world there are four seasons: winter, spring, summer, and autumn.

Winter

In winter, the weather is chilly. Many plants don't grow. Some trees have bare branches.

Birds build nests and their eggs hatch.

.... Some animals hide in burrows, away from the cold.

Spring

In spring, the weather begins to warm up. Plants start to flower and new leaves appear on the trees.

Two seasons

Around the middle of the world there are only two seasons – dry and wet. In the **dry** season the weather is hot. When the **wet** season comes it can still be hot, but there is **lots** of rain, too.

In the wet season the rain is very heavy.

Summer

In summer, the weather is warm. Plants grow bigger and trees have lots of green leaves.

Animals are busy out and about.

Birds fly away to warmer places.

Autumn

In autumn, the weather gets cooler. Plants finish flowering and some trees begin to lose their leaves.

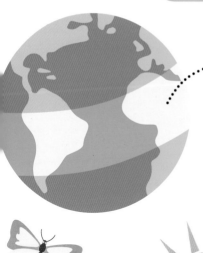

Splendid Sun

Up high in the sky, the **Sun** has an important job to do. It **warms** us up and gives us **light**.

The Sun sets in the west...

Scorching hot

The Sun is extremely hot. It warms up the world from far away. Some places get more heat from the Sun than others.

Plants, flowers, and trees all need sunlight to grow.

Closest star

The Sun is a star, but it's much closer to Earth (where we live) than other stars we see at night. It's so close, it's too bright for us to look at – even when we wear sunglasses.

When the Sun is in the sky it's daytime.

...and rises in the east.

Staying still

Every day it looks like the Sun rises in one place and sets in another. But it's actually the Earth that's moving, while the Sun stays still.

A cockerel says "cock-a-doodle-doo!" when the Sun rises.

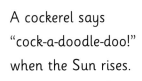

11

What is a cloud?

There are tiny specks of **water** in the air around us. They are called **water vapour**. They are usually too small for us to see. When they get bigger, they group together to make **clouds**.

What's that shape?

Clouds change shape in the sky because the wind blows them around. Spotting shapes is a good game for a cloudy day. Start by looking at this picture. What shapes can you see?

Can you see anything you recognize in these clouds?

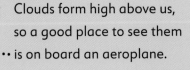

When a cloud is made

When tiny water specks grow cold, they turn into droplets. They bump together and join up to make bigger droplets. Eventually they grow big enough for us to see, swirling around in a cloud.

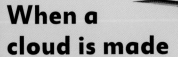

Clouds form high above us, so a good place to see them is on board an aeroplane.

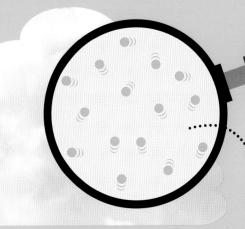

It is very cold high in the sky. The cold makes water specks turn into tiny droplets.

Did you know?

When a strong wind blows rain clouds about, they become one big black storm cloud.

A white cloud turns into a dark rain cloud when it becomes full and heavy with water droplets. This usually means that rain is on its way.

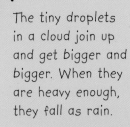

The tiny droplets in a cloud join up and get bigger and bigger. When they are heavy enough, they fall as rain.

Pitter patter

Did you know that **rain** goes round and round in a big **circle?** It's called the **water cycle**.

1. The Sun shines down on the seas, rivers, and lakes of the world. Its warmth makes tiny specks of water rise up into the air.

Our blue world

Millions of raindrops are falling on Earth every second. There is a lot of water on our world!

Earth looks mostly *blue* from space because of all the water.

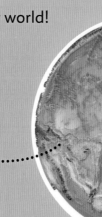

2. The specks rise up and up, and bump together to become droplets. Groups of droplets make clouds.

Follow the circle

with your finger.

3. The droplets keep bumping together. They get bigger and bigger until they are too heavy to stay in the sky.

4. The water droplets fall back to the ground as rain, which runs into the seas, rivers, and lakes of the world.

15

Rain cloud fun

You can do an easy **experiment** to show how water **droplets** work in **rain clouds**. Don't worry though, you won't get wet!

You will need:

Clear glass jar
Water
Can of shaving foam
Food colouring

The food colouring is heavier than the foam. Watch how it sinks through the foam and comes out, like rain from a rain cloud.

1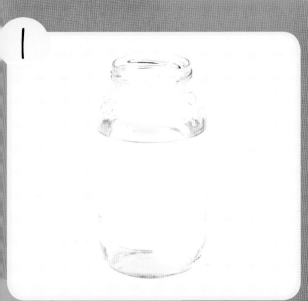

Fill the jar with water but leave some space at the top.

2

Squirt shaving foam on top of the water to make a cloud.

3

Drop food colouring carefully on top of the shaving foam and watch.

4

The food colouring travels through the shaving foam, and falls like rain from a cloud.

Rainbows

If it's **raining** and the Sun is **behind** you, you may see a colourful **rainbow** in the sky.

Can you name all the colours of the rainbow?

Did you know?
The colours of the rainbow always come in the same order. Red is first and violet is always last.

You can see through a rainbow.

18

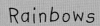

Red
Orange
Yellow
Green
Blue
Indigo
Violet

What makes a rainbow?

Rainbows are made when rays of sunlight shine
through raindrops. Each raindrop splits the rays
of light into lots of colours. These come
together as a rainbow.

Some people think
that a rainbow is
a sign of good luck.

If you walk towards a rainbow,
it looks like it moves further
away. You can never get up
close to one!

19

Icicles form when dripping water freezes.

Brrrrr!

When the weather gets very cold, the **water vapour** in the air starts to **freeze**. That means chilly **snowflakes** could soon be on their way.

How snowflakes are made

High in the wintery sky, tiny specks of water vapour freeze and turn into ice crystals. The crystals join up to make snowflakes that fall to the ground.

This snowflake has been magnified. It looks much bigger than it really is.

Frost

Sometimes the water in the air freezes into ice crystals close to the ground. It settles as frost on the things around it.

You might see crunchy, powdery-looking frost on leaves in winter.

Hail

When it's cold and windy inside a cloud, the water droplets freeze into balls of ice. As they get blown around, they grow more and more layers of ice, and become hailstones.

Eventually hailstones get so heavy that they fall to the ground.

Did you know?

Hailstones can get really big. Some are the same size as golf balls!

21

Icy suncatcher

Make a pretty **ice picture** to hang up outside. It will shimmer and shine until the **heat** of the Sun melts the ice. Then it will turn back to **water**.

How long will your suncatcher last? That depends on how warm the Sun is.

You will need:

Slices of fruit
Cake tin or foil pie tin
Food colouring and water
String or ribbon
Scissors
Freezer

Try adding drops of extra food colouring before freezing.

1

Arrange the slices of fruit at the bottom of the tin. There's no need to be too careful – the fruit will move about.

2

Add a little food colouring to a jug of water. Pour the water into the tin until it is about half full.

3

Cut a piece of string or ribbon, and drape the loop so part of it is under the water.

4

Put the tin in the freezer for at least three hours. Then push out the ice picture and hang it outside.

It's windy today

Wind is air moving. It can gently swoosh along as a **breeze** or tear along as a strong wind.

You might see a windsock fluttering in the wind at an airport. It helps pilots by showing them which way the wind is blowing.

Where does it blow?

It's useful for pilots to know the way the wind is blowing. Flying along with the wind is much easier than flying against it.

You can fly a kite on a windy day.

Watch a weather vane

A weather vane can show us which way the wind is blowing. Look out for weather vanes high on rooftops, where they turn in the breeze.

The weather vane is marked with four directions – north, south, east, and west.

Did you know?

We use the power of the wind to turn wind turbines and make electricity.

Make a weather vane

Make your own **weather vane** to do some windy weather investigating.

Take your weather vane outside. Put it on a flat surface and check it against your compass. The N, S, E, and W should be in the same place as the compass letters.

The way the arrow points shows which direction the wind is coming from.

You will need:

Sheets of card, scissors, felt tip pen, ball of sticky tack, paper cup, pencil with a rubber on the end, paper straw, pin, compass.

If the arrow points between letters, check the direction against your compass. The wind could be blowing south-west or north-west, south-east, or north-east.

W   E

S

Cut out a square of card. Write N, S, E, and W in the positions shown. Put a large ball of sticky tack in the centre.

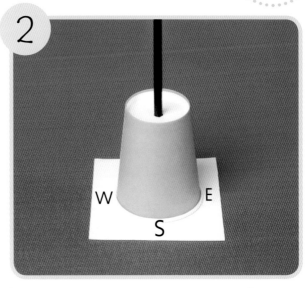

Put the cup upside down on the card. Poke the pencil through the base of the cup and into the ball of sticky tack.

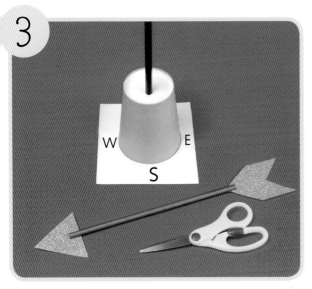

Cut out an arrow head and tail. Make a short snip at each end of the straw. Slide in the arrow head and tail.

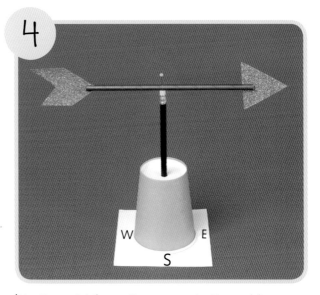

Pin the middle of the arrow to the rubber on the pencil, as shown above.

A stormy night

Crack! Rumble! Watch out for the flash of **lightning**. Listen for the roll of **thunder**. A **thunderstorm** is here!

Storm clouds

These towering clouds form when warm air full of water vapour rises up and meets cold air in the clouds.

Storm clouds can be almost black. They are a good clue that a storm is coming.

28

Here comes lightning

Inside a storm cloud, a strong wind blows around water droplets and hailstones. When they bump together it makes electricity that flashes down to the ground as lightning.

What is thunder?

Thunder is the sound made by lightning tearing through the air. You hear it after you see the lightning because light is quicker than sound.

Lightning is very dangerous. It's best to stay indoors when there's a thunderstorm going on.

A bolt of lightning is a super-fast, super-hot flash of electricity.

Count the seconds

Work out roughly how far away a storm is by counting the seconds between a flash of lightning and a clap of thunder. For every five seconds you count, the storm is about a mile away.

Wild weather

Very strong winds can become **hurricanes** or **tornadoes**. These are dangerous and can **smash** things up.

Horrible hurricanes

Hurricanes are huge swirling storms. The roaring winds of a hurricane can cause lots of damage.

Most hurricanes happen over oceans. The hurricane winds can whip up waves to the size of buildings!

This photograph of a hurricane was taken from a spacecraft high above the Earth. The hurricane looks like a giant spinning cloud.

In the eye of the storm the weather is strangely calm.

Super-whirly tornadoes

A tornado is a funnel of wind that races along, smashing into things in its path. Tornadoes spin out from underneath very tall clouds.

This is the kind of damage a severe hurricane or tornado can cause. ••••

Index

A
Animals 8–9
Autumn 9

B
Birds 8

C
Clothes 5
Clouds 4, 12–13, 15, 16–17, 28–29, 30–31

E
Electricity 25, 29

F
Flowers 8–9, 10, 22
Frost 21

H
Hail 21, 29
Hurricanes 30

I
Ice crystals 20–21
Icicles 20

L
Light 10, 19
Lightning 28–29

P
Plants 8–9, 10

R
Rain 4, 9, 13, 14–15, 16–17, 18–19
Rainbows 18–19

S
Seasons 8–9
Snow 4–5, 20
Spring 8
Star 11
Storms 28–29

Summer 9
Sun 10–11, 14, 19, 22
Suncatcher 22–23

T
Temperature 5
Thunder 28–29
Tornadoes 30–31
Trees 8–9, 10

W
Water cycle 14–15
Water vapour 12–13, 20, 28
Weather vane 25, 26–27
Weather wheel 6–7
Wind 4, 12, 21, 24–25, 26, 30–31
Winter 8, 20

Acknowledgements

With special thanks to Sophia Danielsson-Waters and Hannah Moore for editorial and design assistance.

The publisher would like to the following for their kind permission to reproduce their photographs:
(Key: a-above; b-below/bottom; c-centre; f-far; l-left; r-right; t-top)
2 123RF.com: Anton Jankovoy (Clouds). 3 123RF.com: Aaron Amat (Clouds). 4 Dreamstime.com: Vrozhko (bl) 5 123RF.com: Melinda Nagy (br). 8 123RF.com: Melinda Nagy (bl). Dorling Kindersley: Tim Shepard, Oxford Scientific Films (clb); Stephen Oliver (cr). 9 Dreamstime.com: Gordon Miller / G3miller (cr); Martha Marks (clb); Hai Huy Ton That / Huytonthat (bl); Chee-onn Leong (br). 10-11 123RF.com: Jakobradlgruber (b). 10 123RF.com: Chaturong Gatenil (bc). Dreamstime.com: Irochka (bc/Third Sunflower). Fotolia: Zee (bc/Second sunflower, crb, br). 11 123RF.com: Christian Musat (bc). Dreamstime.com: Irochka (bl). 12 123RF.com: Aaron Amat (b). 13 123RF.com: Aaron Amat (ca); Manfred Thÿrig (tc); Anton Jankovoy (cb). 14 123RF.com: Aaron Amat (cra). Dreamstime.com: Willcao911 (cr). 14-15 123RF.com: Sergey Nivens / nexusplexus (b). 15 123RF.com: Anton Jankovoy (cra). Dreamstime.com: Jojjik (clb); Dmitri Rumiantsev / Rudvi (cla); Lonely11 (c). 16 123RF.com: Aaron Amat (Clouds). 18 123RF.com: Filmfoto (cr). 18-19 123RF.com: Iakov Kalinin (b). 19 123RF.com: Filmfoto (cr). Getty Images: Mike Kemp (bc). 20 Dreamstime.com: Rita Jayaraman / Margorita (cr). 21 123RF.com: Taina Sohlman (ca). Dreamstime.com: Rumos (tl). 24 123RF.com: Stanislav Pepeliaev. 25 Dreamstime.com: Andreykuzmin (br). 28-29 123RF.com: NejroN. 30-31 123RF.com: Adrian Hillman. Dorling Kindersley: NASA / digitaleye / Jamie Marshall (c). 30 Dreamstime.com: Zacarias Pereira Da Mata / Mpz@sapo.pt (br). 31 Dreamstime.com: R. Gino Santa Maria / Shutterfree (clb); Victor Zastol'skiy / Vicnt (r). 32 123RF.com: Manfred Thÿrig (tc).
Cover images: Front: 123RF.com: Aaron Amat c, Fotolia: Zee cb

All other images © Dorling Kindersley
For further information see: www.dkimages.com